# Law of Constantine respecting piety toward God and the Christian Religion

## by

## Constantine

## Rise of Douai

ISBN-13: 978-1517147235

ISBN-10: 1517147239

# Introduction

Constantine the Great (Latin: Flavius Valerius Aurelius Constantinus Augustus; 27 February c. 272 AD - 22 May 337 AD), also known as Constantine I or Saint Constantine (in the Orthodox Church as Saint Constantine the Great, Equal-to-the-Apostles), was a Roman Emperor from 306 to 337 AD of Illyrian ancestry. Constantine was the son of Flavius Valerius Constantius, a Roman army officer, and his consort Helena. His father became Caesar, the deputy emperor in the west in 293 AD. Constantine was sent east, where he rose through the ranks to become a military tribune under the emperors Diocletian and Galerius. In 305, Constantius was raised to the rank of Augustus, senior western emperor, and Constantine was recalled west to campaign under his father in Britannia. Acclaimed as emperor by the army at Eboracum (Modern-day York) after his father's death in 306 AD, Constantine emerged victorious in a series of civil wars against the emperors Maxentius and Licinius to become sole ruler of both west and east by 324 AD.

As emperor, Constantine enacted many administrative, financial, social, and military reforms to strengthen the empire. The government was restructured and civil and military authority separated. A new gold coin, the solidus, was introduced to combat inflation. It would become the standard for Byzantine and European currencies for more than a thousand years. The first Roman emperor to claim conversion to Christianity,

Constantine played an influential role in the proclamation of the Edict of Milan in 313, which decreed tolerance for Christianity in the empire. He called the First Council of Nicaea in 325, at which the Nicene Creed was professed by Christians. In military matters, the Roman army was reorganised to consist of mobile field units and garrison soldiers capable of countering internal threats and barbarian invasions. Constantine pursued successful campaigns against the tribes on the Roman frontiers—the Franks, the Alamanni, the Goths, and the Sarmatians—even resettling territories abandoned by his predecessors during the turmoil of the previous century.

# Law of Constantine respecting piety toward God and the Christian Religion

## Constantine To The Inhabitants Of Palestine

VICTOR CONSTANTINUS, MAXIMUS AUGUSTUS to the inhabitants of the province of Palestine.

To all who entertain just and sound sentiments respecting the character of the Supreme Being, it has long been most clearly evident, and beyond the possibility of doubt, how vast a difference there has ever been between those who maintain a careful observance of the hallowed duties of the Christian religion, and those who treat this religion with hostility or contempt. But at this present time, we may see by still more manifest proofs, and still more decisive instances, both how unreasonable it were to question this truth, and how mighty is the power of the Supreme God: since it appears that they who faithfully observe His holy laws, and shrink from the transgression of His commandments, are rewarded with abundant blessings, and are endued with well-grounded hope as well as ample power for the accomplishment of their undertakings. On the other hand, they who have cherished impious sentiments have experienced results corresponding to their evil choice. For how is it to be expected that any blessing would be obtained by one who neither desired to acknowledge nor duly to worship that God who is the source of all blessing? Indeed, facts themselves are a confirmation of what I say. "FOR certainly any one who will mentally retrace the course of events from the earliest period down to the present time, and will reflect on what has occurred in past ages, will find that all who have made justice and probity the basis of their conduct, have not only carried their undertakings to a successful issue, but have gathered, as it were, a store of sweet fruit as the produce of this pleasant root. Again, whoever observes the career of those who have been bold in the practice of oppression or injustice; who have either directed their senseless fury against God himself, or have conceived no kindly feelings towards their fellow-men, but have dared to afflict them with exile, disgrace, confiscation, massacre, or other miseries of the like kind, and all this without any sense of compunction, or wish to direct thoughts to a better course, will find that such men have received a recompense proportioned to their crimes. And these are results which might naturally and reasonably be expected to ensue? "For whoever have addressed themselves with integrity of purpose to any course of action, keeping the fear of God continually before their thoughts, and preserving an unwavering faith in him, without allowing present fears or dangers to outweigh their hope of future blessings--such persons, though for a season they may have experienced painful trials, have borne their afflictions lightly, being supported by the belief of greater rewards in store for them; and their character has acquired a brighter luster in proportion to the severity of their past sufferrings. With regard, on the other hand, to those who have either dishonorably slighted the principles of justice, or refused to acknowledge the Supreme God themselves, and yet have dared to subject others who have faithfully maintained his worship to the most cruel insults and punishments; who have failed equally to recognize their own wretchedness in oppressing others on such grounds, and the happiness and blessing of those who preserved their devotion to God even in the midst of such sufferings: with regard, I say, to such men, many a time have their armies been slaughtered, many a time have they been put to flight; and their warlike preparations have ended in total ruin and defeat. "From the causes I have described, grievous wars arose, and destructive devastations. Hence followed a scarcity of the common necessaries of life, and a crowd of consequent miseries: hence, too, the authors of these impieties have either met a disastrous death of extreme suffering, or have dragged out an ignominious existence, and confessed it to be worse than death itself, thus receiving as it were a measure of punishment proportioned to the heinousness of their crimes. For each experienced a degree of calamity according to the blind fury with which he had been led to combat, and as he thought, defeat the Divine will: so that they not only felt the pressure of the ills of this present life, but were tormented also by a most lively apprehension of punishment in the future world.

AND now, with such a mass of impiety oppressing the human race, and the commonwealth in danger of being utterly destroyed, as if by the agency of some pestilential disease, and therefore needing powerful and effectual aid; what was the relief, and what the remedy which the Divinity devised for these evils? (And by Divinity is meant the one who is alone and truly God, the possessor of almighty and eternal power: and surely it cannot be deemed arrogance in one who has received benefits from God, to acknowledge them in the loftiest terms of praise.) I myself, then, was the instrument whose services He chose, and esteemed suited for the accomplishment of his will. Accordingly, beginning at the remote Britannic ocean, and the regions where, according to the law of nature, the sun sinks beneath the horizon, through the aid of divine power I banished and utterly removed every form of evil which prevailed, in the hope that the human race, enlightened through my instrumentality, might be recalled to a due observance of the holy laws of God, and at the same time our most blessed faith might prosper under the guidance of his almighty hand. "I said, under the guidance of his hand; for I would desire never to be forgetful of the gratitude due to his grace. Believing, therefore, that this most excellent service had been confided to me as a special gift, I proceeded as far as the regions of the East, which, being under the pressure of severer calamities, seemed to demand still more effectual remedies at my hands. At the same time I am most certainly persuaded that I myself owe my life, my every breath, in short, my very inmost and secret thoughts, entirely to the favor of the Supreme God. Now I am well aware that they who are sincere in the pursuit of the heavenly hope, and have fixed this hope in heaven itself as the peculiar and predominant principle of their lives, have no need to depend on human favor, but rather have enjoyed higher honors in proportion as they have separated themselves from the inferior and evil things of this earthly existence. Nevertheless I deem it incumbent on me to remove at once and most completely from all such persons the hard necessities laid upon them for a season, and the unjust inflictions under which they have suffered, though free from any guilt or just liability. For it would be strange indeed, that the fortitude and constancy of soul displayed by such men should be fully apparent during the reign of those whose first object it was to persecute them on account of their devotion to God, and yet that the glory of their character should not be more bright and blessed, under the administration of a prince who is His servant. "LET all therefore who have exchanged their country for a foreign land, because they would not abandon that reverence and faith toward God to which they had devoted themselves with their whole hearts, and have in consequence at different times been subject to the cruel sentence of the courts; together with any who have been enrolled in the registers of the public courts though in time past exempt from such office let these, I say, now render thanks to God the Liberator of all, in that they are restored to their hereditary property, and their wonted tranquility. Let those also who have been despoiled of their goods, and have hitherto passed a wretched existence, mourning under the loss of all that they possessed, once more be restored to their former homes, their families, and estates, and receive with joy the bountiful kindness of God.

FURTHERMORE, it is our command that all those who have been detained in the islands against their will should receive the benefit of this present provision; in order that they who will now have been surrounded by rugged mountains and the encircling barrier of the ocean, being now set free from that gloomy and desolate solitude, may fulfill their fondest wish by revisiting their dearest friends. Those, too, who have prolonged a miserable life in the midst of abject and wretched squalor, welcoming their restoration as an unlooked-for gain, and discarding henceforth all anxious thoughts, may pass their lives with us in freedom from all fear. For that any one could live in a state of fear under our government, when we boast and believe ourselves to be the servants of God, would surely be a thing most extraordinary even to hear of, and quite incredible; and our mission is to rectify the errors of the others. "AGAIN, with regard to those who have been condemned either to the grievous labor of the mines, or to service in the public works, let them enjoy the sweets of leisure in place of these long-continued toils, and henceforth lead a far easier life, and more accordant with the wishes of their hearts, exchanging the incessant hardships of their tasks for quiet relaxation. And if any have forfeited the common privilege of liberty, or have unhappily suffered dishonor, let them hasten back every one to the country of his nativity, and resume with becoming joy their former positions in society, from which they have been as it were separated by long residence abroad.

ONCE more, with respect to those who had previously been preferred to any military distinction, of which they were afterwards deprived, for the cruel and unjust reason that they chose rather to acknowledge their allegiance to God than to retain the rank they held; we leave them perfect liberty of choice, either to occupy their former stations, should they be content again to engage in military service, or after an honorable discharge, to live in undisturbed tranquility. For it is fair and consistent that men who have displayed such magnanimity and fortitude in meeting the perils to which they have been exposed, should be allowed the choice either of enjoying peaceful leisure, or resuming their former rank. "LASTLY, if any have wrongfully been deprived of the privileges of noble lineage, and subjected to a judicial sentence which has consigned them to the women's apartments and to the linen making, there to undergo a cruel and miserable labor, or reduced them to servitude for the benefit of the public treasury, without any exemption on the ground of superior birth; let such persons, resuming the honors they had previously enjoyed, and their proper dignities, henceforward exult in the blessings of liberty, and lead a glad life. Let the free man, too, by some injustice and inhumanity, or even madness, made a slave, who has felt the sudden transition from liberty to bondage, and oftentimes bewailed his unwonted labors, return to his family once more a free man in virtue of this our ordinance, and seek those employments which befit a state of freedom; and let him dismiss from his remembrance those services which he found so oppressive, and which so ill became his condition. Nor must we omit to notice those estates of which individuals have been deprived on various pretenses. For if any of those who have engaged with dauntless and resolute determination in the noble and divine conflict of martyrdom have also been stripped of their fortunes; or if the same has been the lot of the confessors, who have won for

14

themselves the hope of eternal treasures; or if the loss of property has befallen those who were driven from their native land because they would not yield to the persecutors, and betray their faith; lastly, if any who have escaped the sentence of death have yet been despoiled of their worldly goods; we ordain that the inheritances of all such persons be transferred to their nearest kindred. And whereas the laws expressly assign this right to those most nearly related, it will be easy to ascertain to whom these inheritances severally belong. And it is evidently reasonable that the succession in these cases should belong to those who would have stood in the place of nearest affinity, had the deceased experienced a natural death. "But should there be no surviving relation to succeed in due course to the property of those above-mentioned, I mean the martyrs, or confessors, or those who for some such cause have been banished from their native land; in such cases we ordain that the church locally nearest in each instance shall succeed to the inheritance. And surely it will be no wrong to the departed that that church should be their heir, for whose sake they have endured every extremity of suffering. We think it necessary to add this also, that in case any of the above-mentioned persons have donated any part of their property in the way of free gift, possession of such property shall be assured, as is reasonable, to those who have thus received it.

AND that there may be no obscurity in this our ordinance, but every one may readily apprehend its requirements, let all men hereby know that if they are now maintaining themselves in possession of a piece of land, or a house, or garden, or anything else which had appertained to the before-mentioned persons, it will be good and advantageous for them to acknowledge the fact, and make restitution with the least possible delay. On the other hand, although it should appear that some individuals have reaped abundant profits from this unjust possession, we do not consider that justice demands the restitution of such profits. They must, however, declare explicitly what amount of benefit they have thus derived, and from what sources, and entreat our pardon for this offense; in order that their past covetousness may in some measure be atoned for, and that the Supreme God may accept this compensation as a token of contrition, and be pleased graciously to pardon the sin.

BUT it is possible that those who have become masters of such property (if it be right or possible to allow them such a title) will assure us by way of apology for their conduct, that it was not in their power to abstain from this appropriation at a time when a spectacle of misery in all its forms everywhere met the view; when men were cruelly driven from their homes, slaughtered without mercy, thrust forth without remorse: when the confiscation of the property of innocent persons was a common thing, and when persecutions and property seizures were unceasing. If any defend their conduct by such reasons as these, and still persist in their avaricious temper, they shall be made sensible that such a course will bring punishment on themselves, and all the more because this correction of evil is the very characteristic of our service to the Supreme God. So that it will henceforth be dangerous to retain what dire necessity may in time past have compelled men to take; especially because it is in any case incumbent on us to discourage covetous desires, both by persuasion, and by warning examples. "Nor shall the treasury itself, should it have any of the things we have spoken of, be permitted to keep them; but, without venturing as it were to raise its voice against the holy churches, it shall justly relinquish in their favor what it has for a time unjustly retained. We ordain, therefore, that all things whatsoever which shall appear righteously to belong to the churches, whether the property consist of houses or fields and gardens, or whatever the nature of it may be, shall be restored in their full value and integrity, and with undiminished right of possession. "Again, with respect to those places which are honored in being the depositories of the remains of martyrs, and continue to be memorials of their glorious departure; how can we doubt that they rightly belong to the churches, or refrain from issuing our injunction to that effect? For surely there can be no better liberality, no labor more pleasing or profitable, than to be thus employed under the guidance of the Divine Spirit, in order that those things which have been appropriated on false pretenses by unjust and wicked men, may be restored, as justice demands, and once more secured to the holy churches. "AND since it would be wrong in a provision intended to include all cases, to pass over those who have either procured any such property by right of purchase from the treasury, or have retained it when conveyed to them in the form of a gift; let all who have thus rashly indulged their insatiable thirst of gain be assured that, although by daring to make such purchases they have done all in their power to alienate our clemency from themselves, they shall nevertheless not fail of obtaining it, so far as is possible and consistent with propriety in each case. So much then is determined. "AND now, since it appears by the clearest and most convincing evidence, that the miseries which erewhile oppressed the entire human race are now banished from every part of the world, through the power of Almighty God, and at the same time the counsel and aid which he is pleased on many occasions to administer through our agency; it remains for all, both individually and unitedly, to observe and seriously consider how great this power and how efficacious this grace are, which have annihilated and utterly destroyed this generation, as I may call them, of most wicked and evil men; have restored joy to the good, and diffused it over all countries; and now guarantee the fullest authority both to honor the Divine law as it should be honored, with all reverence, and pay due observance to those who have dedicated themselves to the service of that law. These rising as from some dark abyss and, with an enlightened knowledge of the present course of events, will henceforward render to its precepts that becoming reverence and honor which are consistent with their pious character. Let this ordinance be published in our Eastern provinces.

# THE END

**RISE OF DOUAI**

RISE OF DOUAI

TWITTER : @RISEOFDOUAI

SIGHT BY ELSIE BENEDICT (PAPERBACK) ISBN-10: 1480081272

- THE ART OF WAR BY MR SUN TZU (PAPERBACK) ISBN-10: 1480082007
- MACBETH BY MR WILLIAM SHAKESPEARE (PAPERBACK) ISBN-10: 1480060682
- A CHRISTMAS CAROL BY MR CHARLES DICKENS ISBN-10: 1481194755
- CREATING CAPITAL: MONEY-MAKING AS AN AIM IN BUSINESS BY MR FREDRICK L LIPMAN ISBN-10: 1481158996
- GETTING GOLD: A PRACTICAL TREATISE FOR PROSPECTORS, MINERS, AND STUDENTS BY MR JOSEPH COLIN FRANCIS JOHNSON ISBN-10: 1481090984
- THE INTERPRETATION OF DREAMS BY MR SIGMUND FREUD ISBN-10: 1481134558
- THE COMMUNIST MANIFESTO BY MR KARL MARX AND MR FRIDRICK ENGLES ISBN-10:

1480112445

- THE PRINCE BY MR NICCOLO MACHIAVELLI ISBN-10: 1480119601
- THE WAY TO WEALTH BY MR BENJAMIN FRANKLIN ISBN-10: 1480099651
- THE ART OF MONEY GETTING - OR GOLDEN RULES FOR MAKING MONEY (SUCCESS PRINCIPLES) BY MR PHINEAS TAYLOR BARNUM ISBN-10: 1480138622

Twitter : **@RiseofDouai**

Made in the USA
Las Vegas, NV
08 September 2021